# Chan Master Miao Tian's Book of Wisdom

*and*

*The Guide to Heart Chan Meditation*

## Chan Master Wu Jue Miao Tian

The 85th Patriarch of Chan Buddhism

*To all seekers on the spiritual path*

Visit American Zen Association – Heart Chan, a California registered 501(c)(3) non-profit organization, at: www.heartchan.org

Email all inquiries to the Editor: yjrchang@gmail.com

Printed in the United States of America

ISBN 978-0-557-18866-6

# Contents

# Foreword

This book contains selections of Chan Master Wu Jue Miao Tian's teachings from various occasions over the years from 1983 to 2009. The contents presented in this book are the English translation of the original Chinese texts and DVD lectures mainly from three sources plus some additional ones. These three main sources, each assigned a literally translated title from its original Chinese, include: *Chan and Its Life Force*, *Introduction to Chan Meditation*, and *Heart Chan Meditation Lectures*. To facilitate reference to the original text for Chinese readers as well as to affirm fidelity, all of the selected essays in this book are presented with their source clearly indicated under the title.

Chan Master Miao Tian is the 85th Patriarch of Chan Buddhism and the enlightened spiritual teacher of the Chan School based in Taiwan. He has dedicated his life to bringing to the world the authentic, orthodox teachings of the Buddha (Shakyamuni or Gautama Buddha) which is nearly lost today. The profound and personal realization of the Truth has brought to his awareness that the inner cultivation and peace through the practice of Chan holds the key to the success of humanity as a whole. Witnessing many atrocities of the past and disasters of the present, he has confirmed his grand undertaking as a spiritual leader and is fervently calling for wider involvement and support.

While Buddhist terms are used in all of Chan Master Miao Tian's teachings, they are used simply for convenience and are not meant to be a religious cage that confines the teachings. The teachings are targeted at people of different backgrounds, color, or race who share both the love and compassion and the vision of a more peaceful world. On this common ground, any differentiation based on religion and creed is completely unnecessary and irrelevant to one's spiritual well-being and growth. The ultimate Truth he realized transcends all human terminologies and ideologies.

Therefore, while reading this book, care should be taken when approaching the Buddhist terms. These Buddhist terms, when referenced, are for the sake of conveying the universal message to a particular group of people on that particular occasion. In a different occasion with a different audience, the same message can readily and aptly be expressed in the most suitable way. Therefore, readers of non-Buddhist backgrounds or beliefs should not feel that they are not the intended audience of this book. In fact, everyone *is* the intended audience of this book. Apparent attempts at breaking the religious barriers and bringing all major religions together are made in essays such as *Chan as a Religion*. In other essays new perspectives and interpretations of terminology associated with particular religions are provided, as in *Heaven in Your Heart* and *Heaven and Hell*, with the aim of exploring similarities and seeking unification between religions.

The book is comprised of two parts. *The Words of Wisdom* collects the teaching on Chan itself and its daily-life application to self-development of compassion, love, and peacefulness. The organization of this part bears no strict logical order and each essay may be read independently. *The Heart of Practice* contains the basic guidance to Heart Chan meditation, which is aimed at helping a practitioner gain basic familiarity with its techniques and benefits. The essays in this part are related to each other, and are suggested to be read in the order presented.

# Editor's Note and Acknowledgements

Over the past eight years or so, I have had the great fortune to practice Heart Chan meditation with Chan Master Miao Tian. I have also had the great fortune to understand his teaching first-hand in Chinese. As teaching and practice are the two legs necessary for walking the spiritual path, I felt that this great fortune has been exponentially enlarged by my access to both.

Since most of the teachings of Chan Master Miao Tian were offered and recorded in Chinese, they are not easily accessible to the Western world. Numerous efforts have been made by many voluntary practitioners to resolve this language barrier by translating the teachings into English. The translated manuscripts, however, are largely scattered in different places and hands and are not in the form as accessible and replicable as a book.

That was the motivation behind the birth of this book.

The materials presented in this book are mostly adapted from the recordings and transcripts of public lectures given by Chan Master Miao Tian. In the process of translating and editing, I have made attempts to look beyond the semantic differences between the Chinese and the English language. Yet in the meantime, I also tried to make the contents in this book as faithful to the original as possible. The result is a translated version that retains its original spoken style, and respects its cultural background and references yet is not limited by them. This book is meant to be read beyond intellectual reasoning and into the wisdom domain in the reader's heart.

I would like to thank many practitioners who generously invested their time in undertaking the task of translation: Jessica Lin, Shilo Chou,

Zhenyao Mo, Jue Miao Jing Ming, Billy Yang, Andrea Wu, Yi-Chun Liu, Yi-ping Chang, Tracy Lee, and others. Thanks to Shilo Chou for editing the early drafts of the book and providing very helpful suggestions on the contents of the book. My appreciation to Billy Yang, Tracy Lee, Zhenyao Mo, Harry Soo, and Donna Obeid for reading the finished manuscript and offering their valuable insights on its revision. I thank Ryan Frisinger for writing a beautiful poem for the back cover of the book. Special thanks to Jue Miao Young Lien and Jue Miao Jing Ming for their encouragement and warmth.

And great thanks to my wife, Yi-ping, for supporting me during the long process of translating, editing, and proofreading. She is also credited for the cover design and book formatting.

Finally, I would like to express my deep gratitude to Chan Master Miao Tian for his teachings and granting me the opportunity to work on this project. Both are indispensable to the incubation of this book.

Ronald Y. Chang, Ph.D.
Los Angeles, April 2009

# Part One

# The Words of Wisdom

# The Meaning of Chan

*(adapted from "Chan and Its Life Force," p. 114)*

The Chinese word *Chan* originates from the Sanskrit word *dhyana*, meaning *quiet meditation*. Most people think of Chan as sitting quietly or sitting meditation. This is however only the external form of Chan. The essence of Chan rests in cultivating the absolute wisdom in meditation and witnessing the absolute Truth with the absolute wisdom.

So, sitting meditation is less about sitting and more about meditation. Sitting meditation is not just sitting quietly, nor is it sitting for the sake of sitting. Sitting meditation is to meditate on the true nature of reality and witness the absolute wisdom. Through sitting meditation practice, the Truth is realized first-hand at the heart. This is very different from intellectual understanding.

# The Life Force of the Universe

*(adapted from "Chan and Its Life Force," p. 48-49)*

What is Chan? The entire body of the universe is Chan. Chan is the supreme life force and wisdom of the universe, in the form of light that fills up the entire universe.

Some forms of light are invisible, while others are visible such as stars twinkling. This celestial and cosmic light has a huge life force that can transform an ordinary person to a saint, an intellect to a sage, and a follower to a leader. The question is whether you know how to use it.

Most people think of Chan as meditation. This understanding is a misconception about Chan. In fact, Chan is not limited to the practice of meditation; Chan is the supreme life force and wisdom of the universe from which all creatures are derived. For example, all the creatures on earth—plants and animals alike—rely on the sunlight and solar energy to sustain lives. If there were no sunlight, there would have been no life on earth.

So your scope and perspective will open after practicing Chan. Most people make judgments from a subjective point of view, based on his or her own limited knowledge. Chan practitioners, instead, have a more holistic point of view that incubates a more objective opinion and decision.

# The Abundant Life Force

*(adapted from "Chan and Its Life Force," p. 102-103)*

Chan is the abundant universal life force. This life force supports and contributes to all lives and physical forms. For example, in the solar system, the sun provides abundant life elements that are far beyond human being's comprehension. The sun releases its solar energy to the earth to sustain all living creatures on the planet. This is one evidence of the life force in nature.

If we can identify the source of the life force in nature, we will uncover the boundless treasures for all creatures to use. We have already observed some success in capturing solar energy with solar cells to generate electricity to improve our living. This achievement should be further advanced by developing next-generation science and technology in the solar energy industry. Inventing more reliable ways of using solar energy to generate electricity is crucial to solving the energy crisis on earth as well as to helping our future civilization. This is one application of the universal life force.

# Life Force and Breathing

*(adapted from "Chan and Its Life Force," p. 67-68)*

If you want to acquire true life force, you need to restructure your physical form first. The analogy is like this: if you want to watch TV shows in a foreign country, you need to get satellite TV first.

Usually we receive the solar energy indirectly through food consumption. Now if we want to acquire solar energy directly from the sun, what should we do? We need to change the internal structure of our physical form.

First, change the way of breathing. We all know that we must breathe to live. Most people breathe through their "chest," that is, breathing into the upper part of the lungs and breathing out. Thus, the life span is short. If we want to prolong our life, we must learn how to do deep breathing, that is, taking the air deeply into the bottom of the lungs so that the diaphragm goes down and the belly expands. Shifting from the short, shallow way of chest breathing to the long, deep way of breathing is the first step to restructuring our physical form.

The second step is to learn to master belly breathing. It is the proper way of breathing for meditation. If you feel out of breath during meditation, try to regulate it until your breath is slow, long, and even.

# Chan Is the Wisdom of the Universe

*(adapted from "Chan and Its Life Force," p. 50-51)*

Let's talk about the wisdom of the universe.

Take the sun as an example. It shines and releases heat without going through any learning process. The innate energy and wisdom of the sun does the work spontaneously. Likewise, phototropism is also innate of plants, without any need of coaching. These are all manifestations of Chan wisdom.

Chan is the "super power" of the universe. If you look at the solar system as an example, you will notice that the moon, earth, and other planets orbit harmoniously following a certain path. They do not run into each other. All creatures on the earth are not tossed into space thanks to the gravity of the earth—the "super power" innate to the earth.

Therefore, the "real face" of the universe is this spontaneity, life force, wisdom, and supreme power of the universe.

Practicing Chan meditation can cultivate this life force and wisdom. Furthermore, Chan meditation can help us harmonize our body—a miniature universe, after all—in a similar way to the greater universe harmonizing itself.

# Cosmic Chan

*(adapted from "Chan and Its Life Force," p. 100-101)*

The universe contains many galaxies and creatures that inhabit the planets in the galaxy. Their existence and change are Chan. In fact, all physical, materialistic, and chemical change and transformation in nature are all part of Chan.

Within the entire universe, all life phenomena, including our daily routines of eating, working, and sleeping, are part of Chan. Once you understand this broad scope of Chan and its spirit, you will have a new and broader perspective on your life and worldview. You will also understand the law of nature that rules all physical beings. For example, the life extension of creatures is such that mammals will beget mammals, and reptiles will beget reptiles. A mammal will not beget a reptile. This is the law of nature, and the Truth. The Truth is Chan.

Therefore, a close look into Chan will reveal the Truth—the ultimate Truth. Science has proven that life is born out of a male and a female. Without each other, life cannot be created. This is the law of nature. Many wonders of modern inventions and discoveries were achieved based on this law of nature, such as the invention of electricity which further leads to many other inventions. This continues to multiply and has collectively built modern civilizations. This is one revelation of Chan.

# Galactic Chan

*(adapted from "Chan and Its Life Force," p. 22-23)*

Our mother earth is one planet among millions of millions of planets and stars in the universe. The earth is connected with other planets in many subtle ways. For instance, the sun, moon, and earth are all part of the solar system and the interactions between them directly influence our moods, even consciousness. During the time when the sun, moon, and earth are in alignment—inducing the strongest influence on living beings—people tend to be more emotional and impulsive. Patients of psychological disorders tend to have a relapse, especially on the fifteenth of the lunar month. Nature also has its cyclical phenomenon, such as the ebb and flow of the tides of the ocean. Chan practitioners should contemplate on these phenomena in nature as there is immense wisdom in them.

Life is created by dual energies, such as *yin* and *yang*. For example, all creatures in the animal kingdom have males and females. Even the earth is no exception—its existence depends on the sun (*yang*) and moon (*yin*).

# Heart Chan—Only the Heart Knows the Truth

*(adapted from "Heart Chan Meditation Lecture 1A")*

What is *Heart Chan*? *Heart* is the Buddha-nature within all of us, which we want to look inward to get in touch with moment-by-moment. *Chan* is the universal life force and wisdom. The core teachings of our Chan School rest in the special way of teaching *without words and formalities* and *directly from-heart-to-heart*. Nothing outside the heart has any spiritual significance—they are simply attachments. Through meditation, the heart is transformed from dark to light, from contaminated to pure, and from small to big. Any mundane matters that bother you should not be treated too seriously and personally. Do not let them contaminate your originally peaceful and pure heart.

Speaking of meditation, it is worthwhile to point out that meditation itself does not constitute the entire practice. Wisdom, an awakened heart, and a clear objective to meditate with are all necessary elements of the practice. Therefore, such practices as reciting sutras without understanding, or chanting mantras without change of attitude towards benevolence, are not Heart Chan. They are merely other forms of meditation.

There are some forms of meditation that will not lead to Enlightenment, no matter how long or diligently they are practiced. Why? The reason lies in the difference between meditating with the *mind* and meditating with the *heart*. If you meditate with your mind and logic, you will not be able to enter meditative state and, as a result, enter into a spiritual world that is beyond the time and space on earth. In other words, you will not be able to witness the spiritual domain which, although indiscernible and intangible, does exist. Without the personal journey from the three-dimensional world to the higher-dimensional Heaven or

Buddhaland, Enlightenment is impossible. Therefore, we should meditate with our heart. When you meditate, try to embrace a joyous heart and a smiley face, much like the happy moment of arriving home from a long journey. In fact, your face—smiling or frowning—reveals everything about the quality of your meditation.

# Chan as a Religion

*(adapted from "Chan and Its Life Force," p. 63-64)*

Let us talk about Chan as a religion. Christians go to church on Sundays for sermons and meet regularly for Bible study in search of the personal connection to and experience with God. They believe that the elevation of one's life and the salvation of one's soul can be attained through these practices. Catholics, in a similar way, look for the individual connection with the Holy Mother through the Holy Spirit. Only those who are with their purest heart can commune with the Holy Spirit and be guided to the Holy Mother. In the East, Buddhists practice by identifying the true nature within them, connecting to the universal Dharma-nature, and eventually leading to the awakening of one's own Buddha-nature. Despite the different terminologies used, the practices of these major religions bear many similarities. All stress the importance of the purity of one's heart and body. All call for an individual's undivided dedication and discourage wandering thoughts. All believe that a safer and more peaceful society is attainable as long as each of us, the element of the society, is in touch with the torch of truth and compassion deep within.

All religions teach morality, kindness and charity. Pastors, Fathers, and Dharma Teachers, regardless of their religious origins, preach ways to transcend our everyday mundanity with wisdom and live a life of fulfillment. A fulfilled life has nothing to do with personal fortune or social status. A person of limited material resources may live a life far more fulfilled and satisfying than a wealthy one. No material wealth or social prestige can bring happiness; happiness only flows from within, from the wisdom of inner peace and contentment.

# Heaven in Your Heart

*(adapted from "Chan and Its Life Force," p. 130-131)*

A true Chan Master is enlightened; all the sentient beings inside his body have been cleansed and liberated to the state of Nirvana. What is sentient being? What is Nirvana? Nirvana is a state of total blessedness, complete release from the cycle of reincarnation. Sentient beings are the organs and cells in our body—heart, liver, spleen, lungs, kidneys, colon, intestines, bones, gall bladder, blood, brain, cerebellum, the third ventricle, and all the germs that exist in the body.

We rely on food to supply energy and nutrients to the body. The food consumed converts into parts of our body, such as muscles. When we die, the foods that we have taken in transform into worms which decompose the flesh. The flesh is sentient being. The body is sentient being. The worms are sentient being. These sentient beings need to be purified and liberated before Enlightenment can be attained.

The so-called "Hell" is suffering—sickness, stress, depression, worries. These sufferings torment us recurrently, thus "reincarnation." Many people do not believe in Heaven or Hell. Yet, look at the famine, refugees, prisoners, and wars—this is Hell on earth. The suffering that people have experienced is Hell.

On the other hand, there is Heaven on earth too. You do not need to look outward for it—it is in your heart. As long as you are joyful and peaceful, this very moment is in Heaven, or Buddhaland. Once you can maintain such a state consistently, you will gradually witness your true self—the Dharma-body—in the form of light. In the language of Christianity, it is the light of the Holy Spirit. It is eternal. Witnessing first-hand the eternal life is the highest achievement in Chan.

# Heaven and Hell

*(excerpted from "Chan School Magazine," no. 7)*

In our life, we should always try to find happiness in suffering, or find Heaven in Hell. This is called the wisdom of life.

What does that mean? In fact, Heaven and Hell are simply notions of our state of mind, which fluctuates as we experience ups and downs in life. During tough times, we should try to look on the bright side and search for ways to liberate ourselves from misery and grief. In other words, we should try to seek Heaven in Hell. How? The key is to maintain a stable, calm, and peaceful mind. Try not to blame the external factors, the unfortunate fate, or things that failed your expectation. Instead, be appreciative of what you already have. You may also want to give meditation a try, as meditation can bring a person the positive energy and mindset needed to defeat misery, grief, and suffering. Gradually as we develop calmness and equanimity through meditation, we will see the light of Heaven in these challenging situations.

As there is Heaven in Hell, there is Hell in Heaven, too. For example, if a person is materially wealthy but is ungrateful and unsatisfied, this person is not spiritually rich. In other words, this person's state of mind and heart is not parallel to the material blessing and thus the good fortune will not last long. This is unfortunate.

So, no matter what the surrounding environments might be—Heaven, Hell, or a mixture of both—what truly matters is our heart and mind. Try to keep your heart and mind in Heaven moment-by-moment. This is the secret to true and lasting happiness.

# Harmonizing Your Daily Life

*(adapted from "Chan and Its Life Force," p. 12-13, 16-17)*

All living beings, including all mammals, crustaceans, reptiles, and invertebrates, experience the four life phases of *birthing, living, changing,* and *perishing*. For human beings, everything—from growing and maturing to living and experiencing happiness, anger, sadness, joy, and various other fluctuations in life—follows this law of nature.

Human beings are born with an inherent wisdom, making them the dominant species in the world. Due to this innate wisdom, human beings have developed many marvelous civilizations.

However, because of our need to fight for survival, we are often too occupied to attend to our spiritual needs. Wealthy people are not exempt from pain; distress and everyday issues are still part of their lives. We can fairly say that worries and pains are always part of life. How can we liberate ourselves from worries and pains then? The key is to have the wisdom to transcend life's challenges.

Every human being has a physical self (*body*) and a conscious self (*ego*). The notion of "I" arises from the conscious self, and produces the desire. The pursuit of desire is eventually a vain quest which exhausts the body and the soul, as human desire is insatiable.

Some may argue that life would be meaningless if there were no desires. In fact, *desire* and *ideal* are not to be confused. *Desire* represents the sensual needs, which are hard to satisfy. An *ideal* is something different—it is the proper view and ultimate goal of life. For example, if we had not been given care and support from our parents, teachers, and society, we could not have developed into an adult. Realizing this, we should reciprocate with care and support to others, without expecting anything in return.

An ideal like this often stems from the compassionate nature within ourselves. No matter where you are and what you do, compassion will always make you a dignified and respected person. A compassionate heart can greatly improve your relationship and your surrounding environment. Compassion is also contagious—people around you will become more benevolent and compassionate because of you.

The purpose in life is to accomplish an ideal, not to pursue a desire. It is my hope that we can all be responsible for future generations, dedicating our lives to improving our environment and the world. This is truly an ideal that we can share and fulfill together.

# Cultivating the Inner Buddha-nature

*(adapted from "Chan and Its Life Force," p. 14-15)*

Everyone has the innate wisdom. One of the main purposes of practicing Chan is to realize and witness this concealed wisdom.

Many Buddhist practitioners do not have a clear objective for their practice. Some mistake chanting as the sole practice, hoping to be ferried to Buddhaland by Bodhisattvas when they die. Others practice for the benefits of their career and wealth. No matter what the goal might be, an undisputed fact is that we all age and deteriorate. Our energy dwindles, eventually to a point where life is not sustainable.

What, then, is the value and purpose of human life? By conventional value, titles, fame, and possessions seem to define who we are. However, a deeper reflection will reveal the higher purpose of life. In fact, we are here to attain a higher goal, one beyond living a good life and having a successful career. Cultivating and witnessing the Buddha-nature within, for example, is one such goal which people often neglect. A Chan practitioner should dedicate his or her life to accomplishing this goal.

# Outside the True Heart Exists No Buddha

*(adapted from "Chan and Its Life Force," p. 186-187)*

Historically, Chan Buddhism is known to teach its practitioners without formality and language. It is the teachings of "heart-to-heart transmission." It is also known to be "pointing straight to the heart," "witnessing true nature," and "seeing Buddha, becoming Buddha." The teaching is not based on languages or doctrines, so you need not be educated in Buddhism or sutras to practice it. Words and languages are forms. As Bodhidharma has taught us, we must not attach to forms:

In Chan, there is no other heart (except the true heart)

In *Ding**, there is no other form (except the true form)

—Bodhidharma, the 1st Patriarch of Chinese Chan

If we are attached to forms, we are seeking outside the true heart. If we are seeking outside the true heart, we will never witness Buddha, or the Truth.

Remember this:

Outside Buddha exists no true heart

Outside the true heart exists no Buddha

---

* *Ding* is a Chinese word meaning stillness.

# Everything under the Sun

*(excerpted from speech "Perspective on the Truth of Life")*

All life forms on earth rely on the sun and its heat and energy to live. If there were no sun, there would be no life on earth.

In other words, the sun is the vital source of energy that all life forms need in order to sustain their lives. For example, plants rely on air, water, and light to grow. Likewise, herbivorous animals such as cows, sheep, and horses rely on grass which grows upon air, water, and light. For human beings, the food we eat—vegetables or meat—and the nutrition we take in are the mixture and refinement of the nature's air, water, and sunlight. Therefore it is fair to say that all beings in the food chain rely on the sun. What makes the food we eat seem so different from its original source is simply the countless chemical transformation processes.

Since the energy and nutrition in all kinds of food are derived from the sun, we may be able to obtain the energy in a more direct way than eating. For example, if we can absorb and utilize the energy directly from the sun, using it to nurture and strengthen our body, we will be very energetic and healthy. This is a purely natural and direct means to acquire the energy that we need to survive.

The remaining question is: how do we develop such an ability? We can develop it gradually through practicing Chan meditation. Meditation calms, tranquilizes, and purifies our body and mind, and therefore enables us to synchronize with the purist and most natural energy, such as the sunlight. With the right methodology and practice, everyone can use the vital source of energy, such as the sunlight, to massage and rejuvenate the brain, eyes, and neural systems.

While our body needs nutrition and energy, we should also not forget that our spirit, or Buddha-nature, needs nutrition and energy too. Just like our body needs sunlight, our Buddha-nature needs light too. It is however a different type of light—so-called Buddha's light or God's light. Sunlight and Buddha's light—one visible and tangible while the other invisible and intangible—are exactly what our body and spirit need. And these two different forms of energy can be gained simultaneously through meditation.

# Sutra-opening Verse

*(adapted from "Heart Chan Meditation Lecture 1A")*

In the beginning of all our formal sessions, we recite the Sutra-opening Verse. Sutra-opening Verse is a poetic verse or stanza that is taken from the Buddhist scriptures, and is a summary of the Buddhist teachings. In our Chan School, which teaches without words and formalities, reciting the Sutra-opening Verse is probably the only "formality." This practice of recitation, however, should not be treated as simply a formality or routine but as a reminder of Buddhism's essential teachings, or Buddhism in a nutshell.

There are three different Sutra-opening Verses in our Chan School. Let's talk about two of them. The first one is for beginners:

The supreme, profound yet exquisite Dharma,

Rarely encountered in generations.

I listen, absorb, and uphold,

I vow to witness the Truth of Buddha's teachings.

This verse reminds us to be determined in practice. We vow to grasp this rare opportunity of receiving the profound Dharma to realize Buddha's profound realizations.

The second one is for intermediate practitioners:

Avoid all evil,

Practice all good.

Purify our heart,

Attain Enlightenment.

In this verse, *Avoid all evil* and *Practice all good* are self-clear—they are moral guidance to our daily life. *Purify our heart* states that purification, or non-attachment, is a necessary approach to discovering our inherently pure Buddha-nature. The last one, *Attain Enlightenment*, emphasizes that besides moral guidance, the ultimate realization of the reality—or Enlightenment—also stands at the core of Buddha's teachings. These two Sutra-opening Verses have formed concluding guidelines for our life, practice, and spiritual journey.

# Five Poisons

*(adapted from "Heart Chan Meditation Lecture 1A")*

The first essential teaching of Heart Chan is *purification*. Purification is the complete detachment from Five Poisons—*greed* (or *craving*), *anger*, *attachment*, *arrogance*, and *suspicion*. Each of the Five Poisons forms an obstacle to Enlightenment. Let us take a moment to self-examine our relationship with the Five Poisons.

According to my experience, *greed* is greatly lessened after a continued time of practice. *Anger*, however, may still be a lingering issue for some practitioners. *Attachment*, which includes attachment to bad habits and superstitious ideologies, is relatively a minor issue. Attachment to superstitious ideologies can be trimmed by possessing the right and well-rounded understanding regarding our practice.

The next one is *arrogance*. Moments of arrogance are still a significant part of our life. Same for *suspicion*. Among the Five Poisons, *greed*, *anger*, and *suspicion* are of relevance to all sentient beings whereas *attachment* and *arrogance* belong only to human beings. We as human beings, unless we are detached from all five of them, will not cease to be continually reborn, or reincarnated, because Five Poisons turn the wheel of rebirth. Therefore, detaching from Five Poisons is an important homework of ours as Chan practitioners. In daily life, be aware of the moments of attaching to any of them, and retreat from it mindfully and carefully.

# Precepts

*(adapted from "Heart Chan Meditation Lecture 2A")*

The five general precepts for lay Buddhists are: no killing, no stealing, no sexual misconduct, no lies, and no intoxicants. These precepts, however, are not the most fundamental.

The most fundamental precepts are not "precepts on behaviors" but rather "precepts on intentions." The former is exemplified by the aforementioned lay Buddhist's precepts, and the latter is represented by the so-called "Bodhisattva's precepts." Bodhisattva's precepts represent the complete eradication of Five Poisons—*greed* (or *craving*), *anger*, *attachment, arrogance*, and *suspicion*. Once we attain complete eradication of Five Poisons, we are fully purified in intention, and therefore can aptly and naturally guide our behaviors in accordance with the principles described by the lay Buddhist's precepts. In other words, as our intention guides our actions and behaviors, once the intention is pure and benevolent, so are the behaviors. The Bodhisattva's precepts encompass the lay Buddhist's precepts.

# Three Layers of Obstacles

*(adapted from "Heart Chan Meditation Lecture 2A")*

There are three layers of obstacles to Enlightenment: physical, mental, and spiritual. As Chan practitioners we need to identify, confront, and overcome these obstacles that hinder our attaining Enlightenment.

The physical obstacles can be overcome gradually through Heart Chan meditation. By working on the ten chakras, we purify and energize our body, and as a result, improve our health. The mental obstacles can be overcome through Heart Chan meditation, too. By working on the non-attachment to the Five Poisons, we release ourselves from being enslaved by our mind. The spiritual obstacles, or *karma*, can also be overcome through Heart Chan meditation. Karma is the consequences of our past and current actions, good or bad. To resolve bad karma, we need to do good deeds and reciprocate the good energy and good hearts to beings whom we may have hurt previously and thus planted seeds of bad karma. Buddhas and Bodhisattvas will also guide and bless us in the endeavor, so be not afraid and just do it.

It is worthwhile to mention that Heart Chan meditation practice is twofold—self-practice and assisting others in building their practice. By conducting the altruism of helping others, not only are we content and joyous but we also accumulate merits and rewards in doing such *formless charity* which in turn resolves bad karma.

# Theory and Practice

*(adapted from "Heart Chan Meditation Lecture 1A")*

There are two approaches to beginning a spiritual journey: through theory or through practice. Chan Buddhism is the theory, and Heart Chan meditation is the practice. If you begin with the theory, you want to practice next to actualize the theory. If you begin with the practice, you want to learn the Buddhist theory and principles next to deepen your practice. Theory and practice must go hand-in-hand.

A practitioner should not lean to either theory or practice. For instance, Diamond Sutra and other sutras provide us with wisdom and new perspectives on life, but we should not only read and understand the sutras, but also practice the sutras. Both theory and practice can have immense benefits on the physical and mental health. If you are wrestling with mental struggles, such as depression, agonies, or worries, reading the Diamond Sutra will provide an effective relief. If you are suffering from physical pains or inabilities, Heart Chan meditation will provide an effective relief. In fact, physical and mental aspects of being are interrelated. Through Heart Chan meditation we become more content, peaceful, and joyous mentally. Through understanding the teachings of Chan Buddhism we realize the ultimate meaning of life and can aptly guide our daily life accordingly.

The physical and the mental are two impediments to our attaining Enlightenment. Heart Chan meditation places equal emphasis on removing both impediments as it provides both physical health and mental equanimity. Heart Chan is one transportation for a practitioner's spiritual journey—it takes a practitioner from the realm of suffering to the realm of everlasting bliss. What a practitioner needs to do is to get on the transportation.

# Living a Life to Its Fullest

*(adapted from "Heart Chan Meditation Lecture 2A")*

What is the ultimate purpose of life? Is it eating or working? Both eating and working are indispensable parts of our life, and nothing is wrong with enjoying food and working hard. However, they should not constitute the sole purpose of life and occupy the entire life, as we have higher goals to attain—realize our Buddha-nature and liberate ourselves as well as other beings from all sufferings. To gain a deeper and more personal understanding on this, please take a few moments now to meditate on the purpose of human life and the impermanence of the human condition.

We can live our life to its fullest if we realize the existence of a real self or Buddha-nature within us. Lack of such understanding often leads to a life filled with the endless and vain pursuit of fame and fortune. In fact, material wealth will come naturally if the inner Buddha-nature is bright and pure. If the inner Buddha-nature is dark and impure, the pursuit of wealth will not succeed. The order is important—spiritual well-being first and material wealth second. The reverse rarely works.

The Buddha-nature is unchanging and eternal, yet due to our delusional attachments, it is manifested in various forms of life on the carousel of birth and death. Therefore, to uncover its real nature, we must first practice detachment from the Five Poisons through meditation. We should meditate with our heart, instead of with our mind of logic. We should also practice *formless charity*, such as the altruistic deeds of introducing Heart Chan to friends and relatives, and offering time and space for conducting group meditation. The beneficiary of formless charity is the eternal Buddha-nature. The beneficiary of *form charity*, in contrast, is the mortal body. As a result, the benefit and merit of formless charity is immense and immeasurable whereas the benefit and merit of form charity is small and limited. Understanding this utter difference, we should direct our charitable focus towards formless charity.

# Ultimate Wisdom **Is** Realized through Meditation

*(adapted from "Heart Chan Meditation Lecture 2A")*

The core teaching of Buddhism is generally considered *discipline, meditation,* and *wisdom*. There are however Buddhists who do not practice meditation. They have overlooked the fact that meditation and wisdom complement and augment each other. Only through meditation can one unveil and discover the innate wisdom of our Buddha-nature. Other means are inadequate.

The wisdom in question here is the ultimate, immense, and immeasurable wisdom. It is not the same as knowledge from books. Instead, it is the ultimate realization of the true nature of reality, and it is only obtainable through meditation. Meditation helps you to remove layers of physical, mental, and karmic obstacles, and thereby enables you to find the Truth, the reality, and the real *you* hidden inside.

Without the experience of meditation, the Truth is what we know slightly in our minds but not firmly in our hearts. This degree of understanding is shaky and subject to change; in other words, it is an understanding derived from experience with forms rather than formlessness. All forms and materials in this world are transitory and ephemeral, and therefore not real. Is there anything real then? What is eternity? To witness eternity you need to transcend your mind of logic because the Truth is not in the domain of logic. Therefore, when chanting mantras, you must chant with your heart, not your mind. When meditating, you must meditate with your heart, not your mind. This way, you will gradually transcend forms to enter formlessness.

Meditation is the most effective way to transcend forms. When our thoughts cease to arise and our mind starts to concentrate, we are in sync with the present moment which is timeless and formless.

Meditation is the transportation that can take you from this world of forms to the formless world of Buddhaland. Where is Buddhaland? Where is Heaven? In fact, they are not anywhere outside or distant—they are within your heart. These words are simply metaphors for the state of your heart. To witness Buddhaland or Heaven within, you must first have a pure heart that is not attached to the Five Poisons. Then, as your practice develops, you will gradually realize your own Buddha-nature and eventually attain Enlightenment. Without these goals in mind, all forms of practice—meditation or others—are superficial and superfluous.

# Benefits of Practicing Chan

*(adapted from "Chan and Its Life Force," p. 132-135)*

What are the benefits that come from practicing Chan? First, Chan practice improves your health. The $qi^*$ in your body starts self-regulating naturally. The immune system is boosted naturally. Degenerated cells will regenerate, thereby revitalizing and energizing your body. You do not get sick easily. Furthermore, if you attain a higher level of practice, you may also witness different colors of light, such as red and green. As the mother lights of all life forms, these lights can expedite cellular regeneration and improve your overall health.

Second, Chan practice improves interpersonal relationships. Since Chan practitioners are healthier and happier, they have a more positive attitude towards other people. This helps to avoid and resolve conflicts or friction between people. As a result, more fulfilled relationships with others are established.

Third, Chan practice cultivates the wisdom—especially the universal wisdom—within you. When you are connected to the universal wisdom, you will have a broader perspective and worldview, and are more receptive to different opinions and people. Once you apply this wisdom to your everyday life, work, and relationships, you will find that you have less conflicts with others. In other words, you are more at-ease with yourself and surroundings.

Fourth, Chan practice connects you to the universal life force and power which can only be experienced by Chan practitioners. Chan is not about lecturing, listening, studying, or reading. Chan is about personal

---

* *Qi*, or *chi*, is the invisible life force and vital energy that flows through the human body. Literally, *qi* means air, breath, or gas. Thus the term *qi* includes energy both inherited and derived from air. According to Traditional Chinese Medicine (TCM), the smooth and regulated flow of *qi* in the body is crucial to good health.

experience through synchronizing with the spiritual teacher and his teachings, heart-to-heart, so that the Buddha-nature can be released from the cycle of birth and death to return to its home at Buddhaland.

Fifth, Chan practice improves your disposition. Let me give you an example. Three teachers from our Taiwan Chan Buddhist Association once spent time as volunteer counselors at a juvenile prison in Hsinchu County. Counselors are usually too pedagogical to be welcomed by inmates. Our Chan teachers, however, were received with warmth. During the counseling sessions, the juveniles practiced Chan meditation. They repented for what they did in tears, and opened their hearts to our teachings. Each one became a new person with a better disposition and temperament. Not long ago, we received letters from them requesting more lessons and reading materials on Chan. This is an example of the power of Chan applied to daily life.

# Chan Practice Improves Disposition

*(adapted from "Chan and Its Life Force," p. 136-137)*

Some of our practitioners mentioned to me the issues that have arisen from parenting. They told me that their children were rebellious or delinquent, and even stole money from them. I decided to organize a summer camp for these kids and taught them to sit and meditate. The camp was one month long and we met once a week. After only four sessions, parents reported remarkable changes in their children—they became more caring and respectful. This is the power of Chan—it transforms a person from within.

After practicing Chan, our material desire will reduce. We will be more inclined to buy things only out of necessity, not out of vanity. Some practitioners, before they practice Chan, used to live an unhealthy lifestyle of smoking, drinking, and even gambling. After practicing Chan, they gradually shook off these bad habits and lifestyles as they naturally felt uncomfortable continuing with them. This transformation is natural and is not in a self-forceful way. In fact, in our Chan School, we do not emphasize the *external* discipline; instead, we emphasize the *internal* purification of our intention. Once we are pure in our intention, we will automatically abide by these disciplines on behavior and speech. This is one of the most valuable characteristics of Chan teachings—its applicability in everyday life.

In summary, the benefits of Chan practice are multi-leveled and multi-faceted—improving health, transforming temperament, elevating spirituality, increasing blessings, cultivating innate wisdom, and synchronizing a person with the universal life force. Chan practice is not exclusive to any religions, religious sects, or practitioners. Everyone can practice Chan to cultivate peace in the heart. Together we can cultivate peace in the world.

# Teaching the Younger Generation Wisdom

*(excerpted from speech "Chan and Youth Education" on April 21, 1993)*

Many seasoned practitioners have intimately experienced the benefits of Chan practice: improved health, a focused mind, and a constant flow of wisdom. The beneficial effect of Chan can also be expanded to groups of people. For instance, the wisdom of Chan can be applied in schools to improve the teacher-student relationship as well as the education itself. In what specific ways, then, can the wisdom and techniques of Chan contribute to more effective teaching that balances intellectual, physical, and ethical education?

Dealing with problem students in school requires some wisdom and patience from teachers. It is helpful if a teacher can approach students in a way that is more acceptable and less offensive to them. This way, they will have less tendency to block you from entering their own world.

For example, you may ask your students to sit in a chair with their eyes closed and ask them to observe their heart: "Is it red or black? Is it calm or restless? Is it kind or unkind?" These questions will help them to concentrate and quiet their mind.

Try to let them examine their hearts this way from time to time. Once it becomes a habit, they will gradually be more introspective and caring.

There are also some students who have drug issues. How to help these students rid off drug addiction in a fundamental and effective way is still an open question for school administration.

Commonly practiced solutions such as medication often have undesirable side effects and only work temporarily. In fact, the best way is to teach students meditation. The life force that comes with meditation can erase negative messages—such as cravings for drugs—in the brain. If the negative links in the brain are broken, craving for drugs is also terminated. How does this work exactly, though?

Science has shown that through concentrating the mind in meditation, our brain waves or EEG become more stable, steady, and calm. The more focused you are, the stronger the energy will be generated to elevate the brain waves into the state of light. The powerful energy of light waves can cleanse the harmful attachments in the brain, including the addiction to drugs. Eventually the attachments are completely and permanently eradicated through this process.

Concentration is the key to taking brain waves up to a higher state. Only through concentration can one's mind stop wandering, and only when one's mind is still can the brain waves be transformed into light waves. Our wandering thoughts are the interferences that prevent this from happening. Therefore, one of the very basic practices of Chan meditation is to practice concentration.

# Taking Exams with a Peaceful Mind

*(excerpted from speech "Taking Exams with a Peaceful Mind")*

For students, taking exams is a challenge. In our life's journey, we face various challenges—from the environment, relationships, and obligations. If you can overcome those challenges, you will gain strength and experience. But first you must have the will of overcoming.

The essence of Chan is balance. Its realization in the world is harmony and peace. Its realization in an individual is calmness and equanimity. Maintaining a calm and peaceful mindset enhances one's ability in learning, as when the mind is calm, it can easily pick up knowledge from the readings. Solving homework problems becomes easier and more efficient. Therefore, if you want to have good results in your final exams, try to first practice on a peaceful mindset. The calmness and peacefulness will lead to a clearer and more focused mind which will help you prepare the exams.

A calm and peaceful mind is free from worry and stress. With no worries, your mind is at its best state. On the contrary, a restless and anxious mind creates stress. And stress creates disruption. Disruption occupies the space in your mind that could have been used for studying. How can you be well-prepared for finals then?

Try to maintain a calm and peaceful mind even during hectic times. The busier you are, the calmer you should be. In any circumstance, try to remain calm. This is especially true when you are feeling considerable anxiety or stress. Calmness is something that everyone can cultivate through Chan practice.

# Chan Is the Totality of Your Life Experiences

*(excerpted from speech "Everything in Life is Chan" on March 2, 1993)*

Chan is in everyone's everyday life. The first step to fundamental Chan is to do your job well with complete concentration. Here is an example.

If you own a noodle restaurant, your heart and goal is to please your customers. You want them to enjoy their food and their dining experience. With this in mind, all of your efforts are invested in making noodles that taste like no others in the business. This is ultimately tasted and felt by any customer who comes to your restaurant.

The same principle applies to accomplishing your daily work. Regardless of the goal, you should always put forth your best effort in completing tasks. Within the legal boundary, fulfill the demands of your customers. When you see the smile of satisfied customers, you will also feel happy and joyful. It is a win-win situation.

Chan is the accumulation of the pieces from your life. If you want to be enlightened, you should start from the small things. Start with showing kindness to others from your heart, and think of their well-being before your own. This way, you can harmonize your communication and relationships with your peers and friends.

# Fruitful Realization

*(adapted from "Chan and Its Life Force," p. 115)*

We can apply the wisdom of Chan to our everyday life. Over a decade ago, there was a period of time when I was on fruit diet. One day, when I was meditating, the image of a papaya appeared in my mind. I then realized that it was because I ate a papaya that day. If I had eaten a longan, the image of a longan would have appeared. Same for watermelon. It dawned on me that the smaller the fruits, the smaller the leaves; the bigger the fruits, the bigger the leaves. Papaya leaves are bigger than those of mango and longan, so the fruits of papaya are also bigger. Likewise, the leaves of longan and mango are bigger than the leaves of peanuts, so the fruits of longan and mango are also bigger. I realized that bigger leaves have a bigger surface to receive sunlight and therefore can provide sufficient nutrients to bear bigger fruits. From this observation we can deduce that this growth pattern applies to many other fruits too. Therefore, if we want to improve the fruits, we will want to improve the leaves first. This is one example of realizing the Truth of Chan in meditation.

# Anti-aging: Reconnecting with Nature

*(adapted from "Heart Chan Meditation Lecture 1B")*

Sometimes it may appear that we are completely independent of Mother Nature as human beings. This is however not true. For example, when we go to the mountains or the beach we feel more open and energetic. This is the energy of the nature manifested on the workings of our body and mind. Therefore, one objective of Heart Chan meditation is to reconnect ourselves to the nature, for there is immense wisdom and life force in Mother Nature. Trees, plants, birds, and all other life forms are all qualified teachers in many respects for human beings. For instance, trees can utilize the solar energy directly while we can not. Ginsengs can absorb earth energy directly while we can not. Just by learning to duplicate their functions, even only partially, we will be able to rejuvenate ourselves in completely natural ways.

For instance, you can try to meditate in front of a tree, visualizing yourself as the tree. Abandon your social title, identity, and ego—now you are a tree, a happy tree. Feel what a tree feels, and do what a tree does: absorbing energy from nature and generating life force. Meditate on this functionality and how we human beings can learn to do the same. There is significant wisdom behind the life of a tree as well as other living species for us to learn from. Chan is such wisdom in nature, which can be witnessed through meditation.

The universe is a complex yet balanced and harmonic system. Our body is very much like a miniature universe. If we can balance and harmonize our body's elements—organs, cells, etc.—in a similar way to the universe harmonizing itself, we can slow the process of aging and restore the lost functionality of our body. Meditation promotes anti-aging by replenishing organs with energy and life force, and improving our body, mind, and heart altogether, in the most natural way. As our appearance and health are often the reflection of our mental state, maintaining a joyful and peaceful heart moment-by-moment is the best antidote to aging.

# Part Two

# The Heart of Practice

# Sitting Meditation

*(adapted from "Introduction to Chan Meditation," p. 48)*

Meditation is very popular in both the East and the West today. Meditation has become increasingly attractive to people around the globe as an effective means to combat stress, anxiety, and illnesses. For seekers of the Truth, meditation is also a proven means to attaining Enlightenment, or ultimate understanding of the reality. However, not all people understand how to meditate, and some dismiss it as simply sitting quietly and aimlessly. There are even people who fear meditation out of misunderstanding. They equate meditation with hypnosis and spirit-channeling, and due to fear of being hypnotized or manipulated by external spirits, they decline meditation once and for all.

In reality, sitting meditation is neither mysterious nor difficult at all. It is not hypnosis or spirit-channeling. Instead, meditation is a self-developing method that embodies incredible and powerful potential for healing, cultivating well-being, and attaining spiritual ends. Meditation has a wide range of benefits, revealed in all human endeavors and for all walks of life. To name a few: sitting meditation develops a focused mind that enables a student to study more efficiently; sitting meditation nourishes a better relationship with coworkers, and induces creativity; sitting meditation inspires and encourages more effective management skills. Best of all, these benefits are the product of a simple method. Sitting meditation is simple, easy, and safe to learn as long as we follow a set of traditional and recognized concepts and methodologies. These are introduced as follows.

# Getting Ready

*(adapted from "Introduction to Chan Meditation," p. 50-55)*

Before taking the seat for meditation, some preparations regarding the five aspects of your lifestyle and habits are recommended below.

## 1. Diet

Diet has a direct impact on the quality of your meditation. A healthy and balanced diet bases your meditation on a solid ground of *qi* cultivation and circulation. Eat regularly and do not skip meals. Do not indulge yourself in binge eating or starvation diets—balance is always the best. Overeating will create an unhealthy environment in the body that prevents the stomach and intestines from functioning normally, and *qi* from flowing smoothly in energy pathways. Too full a stomach reduces your energy level and makes you sleepy in meditation. On the other hand, eating too little can't provide sufficient nutrition and energy that you need. Therefore, a balanced diet is always important.

The suggested food portion is about 50 to 60 percent of a full stomach. This moderate amount allows the development and storage of *qi* in the stomach. If you plan to meditate, try to eat afterwards or at least one hour beforehand. This will discourage a sleepy condition during meditation, and consequently benefit you more from meditation.

## 2. Sleep

A regular biological clock is an important preparation for meditation, and this begins with quality sleep. Six hours of sleep is recommended, and a sleep time that falls in the duration of midnight (or before) and 7am is the best. Too much or too little sleep produces a drowsy condition during the day, which disrupts your ability to concentrate your mind during meditation and therefore hinders your potential to enter the meditative state.

Many people today are suffering from various sleeping disorders. Insomnia is often the result of an over-wandering and a non-stopping mind. Therefore, to have a better sleep, try to relax your body and mind before bed—through gentle exercise or breathing—and put your restless mind to a stop. Gradually a good sleeping pattern will go into your system.

### 3. Posture and Movement

Posture and movement in daily life can easily affect the posture in sitting meditation. Four guidelines for a good daily life posture are recommended: walking like the wind, standing like the pine, sitting like the bell, and lying like the bow.

*Walking like the wind* is to walk with agility. *Standing like the pine* is to stand upright without slouching or hunching. *Sitting like the bell* is to sit still without fidgeting (the bell refers to the big bell in Chinese or Japanese temples). *Lying like the bow* is to lie down on the right side of the body with legs bent a little. These four guidelines not only help you to cultivate good postures but also enhance your *qi* and blood circulation on a daily basis. They can help to calm your mind too.

In your daily life, try to keep your words, actions, and intentions pure and benevolent. A positive intention—and consequently positive words and actions that follow—will prepare you for a quality sitting meditation.

### 4. Mind

Concentration is an important practice in sitting meditation. To foster a concentrated mindset, try to practice concentration in daily life. Be present and mindful with whatever tasks you are engaging in, moment-by-moment. This minimizes time waste and maximizes self-fulfillment, which in turn brings you the mental awareness and sharpness that helps reduce the random thoughts that arise in meditation practice. A daily life in full accordance with the present moment is the reflection of a mind that embodies wakefulness and non-attachment.

Another aspect of mindset is our perspective on life. For some people, the goal in life centers around the pursuit of fame, wealth, and power. For others—especially an awakened mind—the goal transcends the material pursuit and rests in the personal realization of the ultimate meaning of human existence: to attain Enlightenment and universal salvation of humanity. This deepened understanding of life also deepens the dedication to sitting meditation, and strengthens spiritual development through sitting meditation.

## 5. Breathing and *qi*

Breathing is the fundamental of Heart Chan meditation. Calm, even, and noiseless breathing builds a solid foundation for *qi* purification and cultivation in sitting meditation. Lack of a proper breathing practice hinders growth and deeper experiences in meditation. More detailed coverage on breathing will be given in the latter part of the book.

Basically there are four different phases of breathing. From short to long, from noisy to calm, and from perceptible to indiscernible, they are: *windy, panting, airy,* and *flowing.*

- *Windy* indicates the kind of breathing that is short and heavy.

- *Panting* represents the kind of breathing that is quick and rough.

- *Airy* shows the kind of breathing that is laborious and abrupt.

- *Flowing* analogizes the kind of breathing that is even, soft, and deep.

*Windy* and *panting* types of breathing signal the unhealthiness of the body. *Airy* type of breathing manifests the disharmony of *qi* in the body. *Flowing* type of breathing is the so-called *Tao-breathing*—an effortless and subtle way of breathing most suitable for sitting meditation.

Breathing can and should be cultivated in everyday life. The purpose of breathing is to develop *flowing* or *Tao-breathing*, which is the refined form of more primitive windy, panting, and airy types of breathing. Only through proper breathing can the benefits of sitting meditation be fully realized. Therefore, breathing is one of the very basics and preparations for sitting meditation.

# Five Tips for Beginning a More Rewarding Practice

*(adapted from "Introduction to Chan Meditation," p. 56-61)*

## 1. Creating a meditation friendly environment

A suitable environment for meditation is characterized by the following features.

*Well-ventilated:* A well-ventilated room is more suitable for meditation as it provides fresh air and oxygen. A poorly-ventilated place is sleep-inducing and therefore not suitable for meditation.

*Temperate wind condition:* A place that is too windy, especially blowing from behind, should be avoided for meditation. Exposing the back of your head to the wind may cause headaches. For outdoor meditation, layers of clothing are recommended to keep your body warm and protect your back from direct wind exposure.

*Quiet:* Any place that is quiet and safe is good for meditation practice, such as a study room or meditation center. Avoid spots that may invite distractions such as spots beside windows or TVs.

*Well-lit:* A well-lit room is neither too bright nor too dim, as neither is comfortable. A well-lit condition creates a conducive atmosphere for meditation.

## 2. Wearing comfortable clothes

Loose-fitting clothing is comfortable and relaxing, and allows better *qi* circulation in meditation. Tight and constricting clothing is not suitable for sitting meditation.

## 3. Picking a proper time

Basically there is no restriction on time for practice. The best time, however, is early morning around 6 or 7am. If you need to leave for work during that time, the before bedtime around 9 or 10pm is also good. The only time that is not recommended for sitting meditation is between midnight and 5am, as this is the time for sleep. The bottom line rests in being in harmony with your body's biological clock.

## 4. Maintaining a good mood

You will have a more rewarding meditation practice when you are lighthearted and joyous. If you are upset or in a bad mood, try to change your perspective on things and learn to let go. Gradually you will have a more positive mindset which encourages a more rewarding meditation experience. Putting a smile on your face is also a useful way to turn the mood around.

## 5. Developing a daily practice

As the saying goes, "Rome was not built in a day." A rewarding sitting meditation is also the accumulation of daily practice. Daily practice is each time an enhancement of your learning, and a renewal of your commitment. In developing your daily practice, be attentive to the fundamentals—breathing, chakra focusing, and *qi* cultivation—as they set the foundation of your practice.

# Posture

*(adapted from "Introduction to Chan Meditation," p. 66)*

Your posture is very important in sitting meditation. A good posture is a dignified expression of your commitment to the practice, and your commitment enhances each time you assume the right posture. A bad posture prevents you from sitting long, and consequently, from entering a deeper meditative state. Your posture deserves careful attention in the beginning stage of your practice, as bad posture is difficult to fix once it becomes a habit.

Your posture also affects the circulation of *qi* in various subtle energy pathways in your body. Good posture enhances *qi* circulation and fosters good health, while bad posture inhibits such benefits and growth. Bad posture obstructs the proper flow of *qi* and as a result, the benefit of sitting meditation cannot be fully reaped.

Good posture is the composition of the proper position of your legs, hands, spine, shoulders, and head. They are introduced as follows.

# Your Legs

*(adapted from "Introduction to Chan Meditation," p. 67-69)*

The first part of posture is the legs. With good positioning of the legs, a balanced and stable foundation is built for your sitting meditation. The leg position for sitting meditation is called the *lotus posture*. There are three kinds of lotus postures: Half Lotus, Full Lotus, and Easy Lotus.

1. *Half Lotus:* Crossing your legs with one leg on top of the other is called Half Lotus. Either leg on top is fine. More precisely, put the foot of the top leg on the bottom thigh.

2. *Full Lotus:* Crossing your legs with both legs on top of each other is called Full Lotus. More precisely, put your left foot on top of the right thigh, and your right foot on top of the left thigh. This is the most dignified posture for sitting meditation, and it is highly recommended that those who can do Half Lotus try Full Lotus. While you may find it challenging and even painful to do initially, the condition will gradually improve as you continue to try. A session with Full Lotus is twice as effective and beneficial as one with Half Lotus. In other words, one-hour meditation with Full Lotus position brings a benefit comparable to a two-hour meditation with Half Lotus.

3. *Easy Lotus:* Crossing your legs as in casual sitting is called Easy Lotus. Easy and convenient, Easy Lotus however does not provide a solid foundation for extended sitting meditation. If neither Half Lotus nor Full Lotus is doable, you can begin with Easy Lotus, and gradually embrace the more stable Half Lotus or Full Lotus as your experience deepens. Note that no matter which posture you practice with, sitting stably is the most important.

Once you assume a proper posture, try to still your body. Stable posture fosters a calming mind, and a calming mind is grounded in stable posture. Understanding this mutual dependency will help you begin a rewarding practice. Let the calmness develop naturally out of your dignified, stable posture.

# Your Hands

*(adapted from "Introduction to Chan Meditation," p. 70-73, 76-77)*

We form a *mudra* with our hands for sitting meditation. There are four recommended mudras, which are all simple and easy to learn, yet majestic and perfect.

1. *Diamond Lotus Mudra:* *Diamond* embodies the quality of determination in practicing sitting meditation. *Lotus* invokes the image of a beautiful lotus flower growing out of the dirty mud, and symbolizes a practitioner's pure, innocent, and sacred heart. Forming the Diamond Lotus Mudra is to put your palms together in front of your chest, with fingers pointing up and the right thumb crossing over the left thumb.

2. *Meditation Mudra:* This mudra is the most common mudra to assume during sitting meditation. You form this mudra by overlapping the four fingers of your right hand on top of the left with palms facing up, and letting your two thumbs gently meet at the top to form an elegant ellipse. You may place this mudra near your navel or on top of your laps.

3. *Great Perfection Mudra:* This mudra is comprised of two hands each posing an "okay sign"; that is, you touch the tips of your thumb and index finger to form a circle while keeping all other fingers together and straight. Place the hands on top of your knees, with palms facing the sky. Great Perfection Mudra symbolizes harmonization and perfection.

4. *Great Dharma Heart Mudra:* This mudra is comprised of two hands forming the Great Perfection Mudra but each hand is placed in a different position. Place the right hand in front of your chest with the palm facing left, and the left hand nearby your navel with the palm facing up.

Once we are ready to begin a meditation session, we demonstrate our gratitude and respect by saluting the Buddhas, the Bodhisattvas, and the spiritual teacher with the Diamond Lotus Mudra. We first form the Diamond Lotus Mudra in front of the chest, gradually raise it to touch the forehead between our eyebrows, and finally put the mudra back to the chest level and bow. Saluting sincerely and gratefully is an important etiquette to start a sitting meditation practice. During the time of sitting, we form the Meditation Mudra or the Great Perfection Mudra.

# Your Spine, Shoulders, and Head

*(adapted from "Introduction to Chan Meditation," p. 74-75)*

Besides legs and hands, we need also to adjust the entire body to form a more suitable position for meditation. First is the spine. You should keep your spine straight and upright while allowing its natural curve. Your spine is the *du* passageway of one of the two main *qi* channels, *ren* and *du*. A straight back allows your *qi* to flow freely and your organs and nerves to be free of pressure so that they can function at their best state.

Second is the shoulders. Beginners tend to tense up the shoulders while meditating. This is not only unnatural but also uncomfortable. Therefore, you should always remember to relax your shoulders down.

Last is the head position. You should keep your head centered, front-facing. Tuck your chin slightly. Softly close your eyes, with your eyesight still looking forward as if you were wearing a pair of dark glasses (the eyelids). This awareness will prevent you from falling asleep in meditation.

You should curl your tongue to touch the roof of your mouth. Make sure you are not touching the back of your teeth. Instead, try to curl your tongue a little further towards the throat to touch the soft and smooth part of the upper palate. This action promotes the secretion of your saliva, which prevents thirst in meditation as well as nourishes the heart according to Chinese medicine. This action also prevents your thoughts from wandering. If you have too much saliva, you can simply swallow it. Always remember to close your mouth and breathe through your nose in sitting meditation.

# Overcoming Soreness and Numbness

*(adapted from "Introduction to Chan Meditation," p. 142-146)*

The very first challenge facing you is probably the soreness, numbness, and pain that accompany your sitting. People often wonder why this sensation occurs only in meditation but not in other daily life activities, and why it seems to become aggravated as the sitting time extends. These are all good questions that deserve further explanation.

Human body is like water. If water is clean, you can see through it; if it is murky, you cannot see through it. Likewise, if your body is clean, *qi* can flow through it easily; if your body is "murky," *qi* cannot pass through it without obstruction. In fact, pain and soreness is the result of this blockage of *qi*.

As your practice deepens, however, this soreness and pain will gradually diminish because your *qi* strengthens and obstructions are removed. The process may be "painful," but is a worthwhile investment—just like the pinpricks compared to the benefit of inoculation. Once this stage is transcended, you will be healthy.

To help you rise above soreness and numbness as quickly as possible, three tips are provided below for your reference.

*1. Practice often*

Practice makes perfect. This is true in learning almost everything, including sitting meditation. Practicing once or twice at the same time daily will gradually ease soreness and numbness. Besides, you will find yourself able to sit longer after consistent practice.

*2. Switch legs*

If soreness and numbness has aggravated to a degree that is no longer bearable, you may switch legs but with your eyes remaining closed so that minimal distraction is incurred. This is however the last resort. If you can, try to deal with soreness and numbness with a strong will. In fact, human body and mind work in such a way that if you have the will to overcome, you will; if you do not have the will to overcome, you will not. Meditation itself is a test and fortification of your will which can transfer to overcoming daily life challenges as well.

### 3. Focus fully

By shifting your attention from the legs and the back (or wherever the discomfort is observed) to something else such as chakras or breathing, soreness and numbness is eased. This demands a full concentration of the mind and will cultivate your innate life force. This life force will dissolve the sensation of soreness and numbness.

# Belly Breathing

*(adapted from "Introduction to Chan Meditation," p. 92-93, and "Chan and Its Life Force," p. 69-70)*

The way of breathing—deep or shallow, slow or fast—determines our longevity. This phenomenon is interestingly seen in nature—the longer the breath, the longer the life expectancy. For instance, dogs breathe shallowly and quickly and thus live only 16 years on average. Turtles breathe deeply and slowly and can live up to 200 years.

Most people are used to the shallow way of breathing—breathing into the upper part of chest and out. This is called chest breathing. This way of breathing is inefficient since an inadequate amount of air is taken in, and as a result, another quick breath needs to be drawn. Chest breathing creates an undesired condition where inadequate oxygen is allowed into the capillaries to replenish the cells and for the exchange of carbon dioxide. Consequently, the full functionality of our organs is not realized. In the long run, our body may age and decay more quickly, and malfunction prematurely.

Belly breathing is a simple technique: inhale and the belly expands; exhale and the belly flattens. We all breathed this way in our infancy. Gradually as we grew up, we shifted our way of breathing from belly breathing to chest breathing. This may be the result of a fast-paced modern life which demands habitual quickness in bodily response including quick inhalation and exhalation. As the stress and anxiety heightens these days, if we can readopt a more calming belly breathing, we can relieve our hectic life. Breathing through the belly utilizes the full capacity of the lungs and reduces the damage of cells. The organs are massaged and cells better oxygenated. It is no exaggeration to say that the whole body will be fine-tuned towards the healthy end just through the practice of belly breathing. This has been witnessed intimately by numerous Heart Chan practitioners whose bodies are radiant with youth, health, and life force.

Belly breathing, as true of any kinds of breathing, is a spontaneous practice: it requires time and effort to do it spontaneously. You can practice belly breathing anytime and anywhere during your daily routine, such as in the office or on the bus. Once you are adept at this skill, you will find yourself spontaneously expanding and contracting the belly upon inhalation and exhalation without purposeful effort.

Belly breathing is also the foundation of building a solid meditation practice. Adopting belly breathing in meditation is conducive to a meditative state due to its subtleness and stillness. The full concentration of your mind in meditation also enhances the oxygenation and nourishment of cells and organs.

# Going Deep

*(adapted from "Introduction to Chan Meditation," p. 95, 98-99)*

Deep breathing is widely known to have a calming effect. It relieves nervousness, increases oxygenation of the blood, and enhances metabolism. Humans are born to breathe; yet, few know that breathing can be refined to improve health.

Our breath tends to be short and unrhythmic when we are angry or anxious. Knowing how to adjust our breath in such situations is crucial, as it can potentially change our mental state. Since breathing is connected with metabolism, deep and rhythmic breathing fosters better metabolism. From a health point of view, deep breathing also expels the carbon dioxide from our body and therefore revitalizes our body and mind.

Compared to regular chest breathing, belly breathing has the following advantages and benefits:

1. Belly breathing makes you look younger because the *qi* in your body is enhanced with vitality;

2. Belly breathing makes you live longer because the air extended to the abdomen helps remove unhealthy *qi* from the abdomen;

3. Since belly breathing is inhaling with belly expanding and exhaling with belly flattening back, it is deeper, longer, slower, softer, and calmer. Thus, it fosters a calming mindset.

# Five Tips for Fine-tuning Your Breathing

*(adapted from "Introduction to Chan Meditation," p. 106-108)*

### 1. Be slow, soft, deep, and long (SSDL) on each breath

Breathing should be exercised through the nose and guided with four principles: slow, soft, deep, and long, or SSDL. The slower, softer, deeper, and longer, the better. Breathing must be performed quietly, as any noise in the action of breathing is an indicator of the unhealthiness of the body. Any noise is a sign of malfunction or disorder—however unnoticeable—somewhere in the body. Your health is also revealed by the quality of breathing in sleeping—snoring loudly and heavily is a sign of unhealthiness. If snoring is bothering you, try to purposefully draw a few deep breaths to relieve the situation.

### 2. Be patient in cultivating the breathing

It takes time to master belly breathing, so be patient. Sometimes you may experience discontinuity and unevenness in drawing in and out the breath, in which case you should try to take several deep breaths to smooth it out and calm it down. Gradually with practice, you will transcend this stage.

### 3. Retain 30% of the inhaled air in the belly

If you inhale ten portions of air, retain three in the belly and exhale seven. The preserved three portions will facilitate the refinement of *qi*. Refined and purified *qi* can supplement your vitality and energy.

### 4. Replace *breath-counting* with *breath-following*

*Breath-counting* is a technique used to help a practitioner focus in meditation practice. Basically you count each breath upon inhalation and exhalation, like insomniacs counting the sheep. While useful, this practice demands your mental engagement at all times, therefore hindering the development of enhanced calmness and relaxation, and preventing a deeper meditative experience. A better way is to perform *breath-following*, that is, following the path of your breath naturally without conscious engagement of mind. This method proves to be more relaxing and spontaneous.

## 5. Use breathing practice to sharpen your sensitivity

Can you sense the traveling and movement of *qi* in your body? If a meditator can develop such awareness of subtlety, the sensitivity will benefit him or her in managing daily life with a calmer and more peaceful attitude. This keen observation within the body will contribute to a more sensible and aware approach in guiding the daily life.

# Improving Your Health through Breathing

*(adapted from "Introduction to Chan Meditation," p. 38-39)*

Each of us possesses an innate *qi* in the belly. When we breathe in the air, the air will mix with and strengthen the innate *qi* in the belly. This fortified life force will automatically be channeled to our organs, tissues, and cells to support and nourish their normal functioning. Meditation may appear sedated externally, but it is quite active internally. Cultivating health through proper breathing is our best and most natural preventive care measure as it is purely natural with no side effects.

Developing spontaneous belly breathing is the most important and basic foundation in learning sitting meditation. Mastering belly breathing will channel your *qi* from the flesh into the tendons, bones, marrows, and nerve system. This strengthened life force will improve your health as well as extend your life. The transformation of *qi* may be too quiet and subtle to be discernible. However, with the sensitivity and awareness that sharpens each time you meditate, you will gradually be able to witness the phenomena that have been working in your body.

# Non-Thinking

*(adapted from "Introduction to Chan Meditation," p. 148-149)*

Meditation is about turning our mind inward on a single focus with full concentration. However, our thinking mind tends to wander and fantasize which creates a barrier to concentrating the mind in meditation. These non-stopping thoughts are the product of our brain activity or consciousness. They are difficult to control and are just as active when we are asleep as when we are awake. In fact, dream is one indication that our brain is still active and not resting in sleep.

How, then, can we put our brain to rest when it needs it the most? A straightforward answer is to simply "turn it off" when you do not need it. This will not only conserve your body's energy but will also prevent loss of memory or Alzheimer's at an early age—an appalling consequence of overusing the brain. With some practice, we can all learn to keep our brain young and healthy by "turning it off" when its use is not needed.

An over-thinking mind will also take its toll on our quality of life. Sleeping disorders, dry skin and poor metabolism due to sleep deprivation are all results of an over-thinking mind. Over-thinking may also reflect in an individual's bad temper and impatience, as well as tenseness and nervousness. These all demonstrate the close relationship between our body and mind.

Meditation is a proven antidote to an over-thinking mind. As evidenced by science, our brain waves alter in meditation; specifically, a pure and peaceful magnetic field is generated in a meditative brain. Immersed in this magnetic field—and its augmented form, light—we will be able to reduce or erase the wandering thoughts. This transformation of brain waves is an indicator of a deepened practice, and will happen only when the regular brain activities cease. The pure magnetic field or light is powerful as it can eliminate negative influences from our consciousness and subconsciousness, such as addiction, impulsiveness, greed, infatuation, fury, and the like.

Therefore, when meditating, try to turn the mind inward and focus the mind. By focusing, thousands of millions of random thoughts will cease, and the body and mind will unify. This is when non-thinking manifests itself.

# Non-Thinking Is Not Sleeping

*(adapted from "Introduction to Chan Meditation," p. 160-161)*

Sometimes people fall asleep when they meditate. It may appear that their mind is blank and they seem to attain the state of non-thinking. However, non-thinking is not to be mistaken as sleeping, as the former is awake and aware whereas the latter is drowsy and unconscious. The distinction should be made.

If you meditate with a tired body, you will fall asleep easily. Your attention will start to wander and consciousness start to fade. Eventually you may fall asleep. If this happens often, try to adjust your mood to be joyful and peaceful before you take a seat. This will discourage any sleepiness.

# Replenishing Your Brain Power

*(adapted from "Introduction to Chan Meditation," p. 39-40)*

We use our brain constantly, even when asleep. The aging of our brain—and its extremes, the Alzheimer's and other severe brain disorders—is one evidence of overusing the brain power.

Our body has the potential to remedy itself and replenish its brain power. But this is not possible if our body and mind do not receive their necessary rest or if they are tense and uptight. Since meditation fosters the development of deep relaxation, it is no surprise that through meditation, the brain power can be replenished.

With ample rest, our mind becomes more alert. Its sensitivity to the bodily healthiness (and unhealthiness) enhances. Issues can be identified and cured at an early stage. This sensitivity is one of meditation's side benefits.

# Ten Chakras

*(adapted from "Introduction to Chan Meditation," p. 110-111)*

*Chakras* are energy spots in our body. Biologically, they are connected to the functioning of vital organs, glands, nerve bundles, and numerous energy pathways in the body. Chakras are also where the bio-electricity is produced.

We have ten important chakras in our body. From the bottom to top, they are: Root Chakra, Sacrum Chakra, Navel Chakra, Life Chakra, Kidney Chakra, Heart Chakra, Throat Chakra, Wisdom Chakra, Dharma-eye Chakra, and Zen (Chan) Chakra. Observing and focusing on these chakras can strengthen and enhance our hormone secretion, metabolism, immune system, and absorption of nutrients, thereby improving our health. As we gradually age and lose suppleness and energy, rejuvenating our body through the natural means of focusing on the chakras is increasingly attractive and useful.

Spiritually, ten chakras correspond to *Ten Realms** in Buddhism. As Ten Realms are the result of good or bad karma, focusing on the chakra will resolve the bad karma associated with the chakra and provide us with spiritual benefits.

---

* Ten Realms, according to Buddhism, are the ten spiritual divisions of the universe. These ten realms are: hell, hungry ghost, animal, *asura*, human, deity, *sravaka* ("a hearer"), *pratyekabuddha* ("a lone buddha"), Bodhisattva, and Buddha realms.

# Focusing on the Chakra

*(adapted from "Introduction to Chan Meditation," p. 112, 157)*

Sometimes we meditate by focusing on one or more chakras. When we work on the chakra, we need to focus our full attention on it. Focusing on the chakra has many benefits. First, it shifts our attention away from pain, soreness, or numbness, and thus helps us to overcome physical hindrances. Second, it strengthens our organs and glands by uncovering their hidden potential. As the concentration deepens, the potential is transformed into a higher form of energy, such as the electricity or light. This will enhance our life energy or life force.

Our ability to focus enhances when the focus of attention goes from large to small, coarse to fine. In the beginning, we may focus on a larger area. Gradually we focus on a smaller and smaller area. Eventually we want to focus on a single point.

When we focus on a larger area, the *qi* is less concentrated and therefore less effective and useful. Once we are able to focus on a single point, the *qi* around the chakra will be very powerful. This can be experimented and experienced by yourself.

# Navel Chakra

*(adapted from "Introduction to Chan Meditation," p. 113, 115, 128-129)*

Navel Chakra is located about three-finger-width or one-inch-and-half behind our navel. It is what the fetus "breathes" within the womb and thus it represents the beginning of our lives.

Navel Chakra is the most important chakra in our body due to its intimate connection to all other chakras. The status of the Navel Chakra will affect the status of other chakras in a way similar to the chain reaction—if the Navel Chakra is responsive, all other chakras will quickly respond as well; if the Navel Chakra is energized, the energy will transfer to other chakras as well.

Therefore, Navel Chakra is the "main switch" of the house of a human body. Just like the main power switch of a house needs to be turned on before home appliances can function, Navel Chakra needs to be "switched on" before *qi* can develop in the body.

However, how do you determine whether the Navel Chakra is switched on? Usually you will experience some sensations around the chakra, such as vibration, warmness, or coolness. These sensations are all indications that the Navel Chakra is switched on.